Alex Jones: A Bio

Alex Jones is an American radio show host and conspiracy theorist. He hosts The Alex Jones Show from Austin, Texas, which airs on the Genesis Communications Network and shortwave radio station WWCR across the United States and online. His website, Infowars.com, is a conspiracy and fake news website.

Jones has been the center of many controversies, including his promotion of Sandy Hook Elementary School shooting conspiracy theories, and his opposition to gun control. He has accused the U.S. government of being involved in the Oklahoma City bombing, the September 11 attacks, and the filming of fake Moon landings to hide NASA's secret technology.

He has claimed that several governments and big business have colluded to create a "New World Order" through "manufactured economic crises, sophisticated surveillance tech and—above all—inside-job terror attacks that fuel exploitable hysteria". Jones has described himself as a libertarian and paleoconservative, and has been described by others as conservative, right-wing, alt-right and far right.

New York magazine described Jones as "America's leading conspiracy theorist", and the Southern Poverty Law Center describes him as "the most prolific conspiracy theorist in contemporary America". When asked about these labels, Jones said that he is "proud to be listed as a thought criminal against Big Brother".

Early life

Jones was born in 1974 in Dallas, Texas, and grew up in the Dallas suburb of Rockwall and the city of Austin, Texas. His father is a dentist and his mother a homemaker. In his video podcasts, he reports he is of Irish, German, Welsh, mostly English, and partially Native American descent. He was a lineman on his high school's football team and graduated from Anderson High School in Austin in 1993. As a teenager, he read conservative journalist Gary Allen's None Dare Call It Conspiracy, which had a profound influence on him and which he calls "the easiest-to-read primer on The New World Order". After high school, Jones attended Austin Community College.

Career

Jones began his career in Austin with a live, call-in format public-access cable television program. In 1996, Jones switched format to radio, hosting a show named The Final Edition on KJFK. Ron Paul was running for Congress and was a guest on his show several times. In his early shows, Jones frequently talked about his belief that the United States government was behind the 1995 Oklahoma City bombing, using the incident to put down a growing "states' rights movement". In 1998, he released his first film, America Destroyed By Design.

In 1998, Jones organized a successful effort to build a new Branch Davidian church, as a memorial to those who died during the 1993 fire that ended the government's siege of the original Branch Davidian complex near Waco, Texas. He often featured the project on his public-access television program and claimed that David Koresh and his followers were peaceful people who were murdered by Attorney General Janet Reno and the Bureau of Alcohol, Tobacco, and Firearms during the siege. In the same year, he was removed from a George W. Bush rally at Bayport Industrial District, Texas. Jones interrupted governor Bush's speech, demanding that the Federal Reserve and Council on Foreign Relations be abolished. Journalist David Weigel, reporting on the incident, said Jones "seemed to launch into public events as if flung from another universe."

In 1999, he tied with Shannon Burke for that year's "Best Austin Talk Radio Host" poll, as voted by The Austin Chronicle readers. Later that year, he was fired from KJFK-FM for refusing to broaden his topics. His views were making the show hard to sell to advertisers, according to the station's operations manager. Jones stated:

He began broadcasting his show by Internet connection from his home.

In early 2000, Jones was one of seven Republican candidates for state representative in Texas House District 48, an open swing district based in Austin, Texas. Jones stated that he was running "to be a watchdog on the inside" but withdrew from the race after a couple of weeks. In July, a group of Austin Community Access Center programmers claimed that Jones used legal proceedings and ACAC policy to intimidate them or get their shows thrown off the air.

In 2001, his show was syndicated on approximately 100 stations. After the 9/11 attack, Jones began to speak of a conspiracy by the Bush administration as being behind the attack, which caused a number of the stations that had previously carried him to drop his program, according to Will Bunch.

On June 8, 2006, while on his way to cover a meeting of the Bilderberg Group in Ottawa, Jones was stopped and detained at the Ottawa airport by Canadian authorities who confiscated his passport, camera equipment, and most of his belongings. He was later allowed to enter Canada lawfully. Jones said about the reason for his immigration hold, "I want to say, on the record, it takes two to tango. I could have handled it better."

On September 8, 2007, he was arrested while protesting at 6th Avenue and 48th Street in New York City. He was charged with operating a megaphone without a permit. Two others were also cited for disorderly conduct when his group crashed a live television show featuring Geraldo Rivera. In an article, one of Jones' fellow protesters said, "It was ... guerrilla information warfare."

On June 6, 2013, Jones addressed international media for the annual Bilderberg conference in Watford, England. He gave an hour-long speech to around 2000 protesters in the grounds The Grove hotel, where has was "rapturously welcomed", "surrounded by cameras and peppered with questions".

On July 6, 2017, alongside Paul Joseph Watson, Jones began hosting a contest to create the best "CNN Meme", in which the winner would receive $20,000. The contest was created in response to CNN releasing an article regarding a controversial Reddit user.

Radio, websites and mail-order business

The Alex Jones Show is broadcast nationally by the Genesis Communications Network to more than 90 AM and FM radio stations in the United States, including WWCR, a shortwave radio station. The Sunday show also airs on KLBJ. In 2010, the show attracted around 2 million listeners each week.

According to journalist Will Bunch, a senior fellow at Media Matters for America, the show has a demographic heavier in younger viewers than other conservative pundits due to Jones's "highly conspiratorial tone and Web-oriented approach".

Bunch has also stated that Jones "feed on the deepest paranoia". According to Alexander Zaitchik of Rolling Stone magazine, in 2011 he had a larger on-line audience than Glenn Beck and Rush Limbaugh combined.

Jones is the operator of the websites Infowars.com and prisonplanet.com. His website, Infowars.com, is a conspiracy and fake news website.

A 2017 piece for German magazine Der Spiegel by Veit Medick indicated that two-thirds of Jones' funds derive from sales of a successful range of his own products. These products are marketed through the Infowars website and through advertising spots on Jones' show. They include dietary supplements, toothpaste, bulletproof vests and "brain pills", according to Medick, amid a wide range appealing to "anyone who believes Armageddon is near".

In August 2017, Californian medical company Labdoor, Inc reported on tests applied to six of Jones' dietary supplement products. These included a product named 'Survival Shield', which was found by Labdoor to contain only iodine, and a product named 'Oxy-Powder', which comprised a compound of magnesium oxide and citric acid; common ingredients in dietary supplements. Labdoor indicated no evidence of prohibited or harmful substances, but cast doubt on Infowars' marketing claims for these products, and asserted that the quantity of the ingredients in certain products would be "too low to be appropriately effective".

On a segment of Last Week Tonight, host John Oliver stated that Jones spends "nearly a quarter" of his on-air time promoting products sold on his website, many of which are purported solutions to medical and economic problems claimed to be caused by the conspiracy theories described on his show.

Views

Mainstream sources have described Jones as a conservative, far-right/alt-right, and a conspiracy theorist. Jones has described himself as a libertarian and a paleoconservative.

Following the 2016 Republican National Convention, Jones and Roger Stone began plotting the removal of Ted Cruz from his Senate seat in 2018 through potential challengers Katrina Pierson and Dan Patrick. Jones supports Donald Trump and has consistently denounced Hillary Clinton and Barack Obama.

Mother Jones has claimed that Jones is a believer in weather weapons, and Salon have covered his claim "that the president has access to weather weapons capable of not only creating tornadoes but also moving them around, on demand." His belief in weather warfare has been widely reported by mainstream media.

Controversies

Jones has been the center of many controversies, such as the one surrounding his actions and statements about gun control after the Sandy Hook Elementary School shooting. He has accused the United States government of being involved in the Oklahoma City bombing and the September 11 attacks. In 2009, Jones claimed that a convicted con man's scheme to take over a long-vacant, would-be for-profit prison in Hardin, Montana was part of a FEMA plot to detain U.S. citizens in concentration camps. Jones was in a "media crossfire" in 2011, which included criticism by Rush Limbaugh, when the news spread that Jared Lee Loughner, the perpetrator of the 2011 Tucson shooting, had been "a fan" of the 9/11 conspiracy film Loose Change of which Jones had been an executive producer.

In April 2017, Jones was criticized for claiming that the Khan Shaykhun chemical attack was a hoax and a "false flag". Jones stated that the attack was potentially carried out by the White Helmets, which he claim are an Al-Qaeda-affiliated terrorist front financed by George Soros.

In October 2017, Jones faced criticism from the media after he was reported to have published some of the first graphic photos of a deceased Stephen Paddock at the crime scene of the 2017 Las Vegas shooting.

In February 2017, the lawyers of James Alefantis, owner of Comet Ping Pong pizzeria, sent Jones a letter demanding an apology and retraction for his role in pushing the Pizzagate conspiracy theory. Under Texas law, Jones was given a month to comply or be subject to a libel suit. In March 2017, Alex Jones apologized to Alefantis for promulgating the conspiracy theory and retracted his allegations.

In April 2017, the Chobani yogurt company filed a lawsuit against Jones for his article that claims that the company's factory in Idaho, which employs refugees, was connected to a 2016 child sexual assault and a rise in tuberculosis cases. As a result of the lawsuit, Jones issued an apology and retraction of his allegations in May 2017.

In December 2015, Jones initially "formed a bond" with Donald Trump, after the presidential candidate appeared on The Alex Jones Show, claiming Jones had an "amazing reputation". During the 2016 presidential campaign, Hillary Clinton criticized Donald Trump for his ties to Alex Jones. Jones said that Trump called him on the day after the election to thank him for his help in the campaign. Since Donald Trump took office, it has been claimed Jones communicates with the President through aides, something which Chief of Staff John Kelly has reportedly tried to block. In June 2017, journalist Bill Moyers claimed that Trump and Jones explicitly "operate as a tag team".

In January 2013, Jones was invited to speak on Piers Morgan's show after promoting an online petition to deport Morgan because of his support of gun control laws. The interview turned into "a one-person shoutfest, as Jones riffed about guns, oppressive government, the flag, his ancestors' role in Texan independence, and what flag Morgan would have on his tights if they wrestled." The event drew widespread coverage, and according to The Huffington Post, Morgan and others such as Glenn Beck "agreed that Jones was a terrible spokesman for gun rights". Jones's appearance on the show was a top trending Twitter topic the following morning.

On June 9, 2013, Jones appeared as a guest on the BBC's television show Sunday Politics, during a discussion about conspiracy theories surrounding the Bilderberg Group meetings with presenter Andrew Neil and journalist David Aaronovitch. A critic of such theories, Aaronovitch implied that they either do not exist or that Jones is a part of them himself. Jones began shouting and interrupting, and Andrew Neil ended the interview, describing Jones as "an idiot" and "the worst person I've ever interviewed". According to Neil on Twitter, Jones was still shouting until he knew that he was off-air.

Personal life

Jones has three children with ex-wife Kelly Jones. The couple divorced in 2015. In 2017, Kelly sought sole or joint custody of their children due to Alex's behavior. She claimed "he's not a stable person" and "I'm concerned that he is engaged in felonious behavior, threatening a member of Congress". Alex's attorney responded that "he's playing a character" and described him as a "performance artist". In court, Jones denied playing a character and called his show "the most bona fide, hard-core, real McCoy thing there is, and everybody knows it." The court awarded Kelly the power to decide where their children live.

Media

The New World Order or NWO is claimed to be an emerging clandestine totalitarian world government by various conspiracy theories.

The common theme in conspiracy theories about a New World Order is that a secretive power elite with a globalist agenda is conspiring to eventually rule the world through an authoritarian world government—which will replace sovereign nation-states—and an all-encompassing propaganda whose ideology hails the establishment of the New World Order as the culmination of history's progress. Many influential historical and contemporary figures have therefore been purported to be part of a cabal that operates through many front organizations to orchestrate significant political and financial events, ranging from causing systemic crises to pushing through controversial policies, at both national and international levels, as steps in an ongoing plot to achieve world domination.

Before the early 1990s, New World Order conspiracism was limited to two American countercultures, primarily the militantly anti-government right and secondarily that part of fundamentalist Christianity concerned with the end-time emergence of the Antichrist. Skeptics such as Michael Barkun and Chip Berlet observed that right-wing populist conspiracy theories about a New World Order had not only been embraced by many seekers of stigmatized knowledge but had seeped into popular culture, thereby inaugurating a period during the late 20th and early 21st centuries in the United States where people are actively preparing for apocalyptic millenarian scenarios. Those political scientists are concerned that mass hysteria over New World Order conspiracy theories could eventually have devastating effects on American political life, ranging from escalating lone-wolf terrorism to the rise to power of authoritarian ultranationalist demagogues.

History of the term

During the 20th century many politicians, such as Woodrow Wilson and Winston Churchill, used the term "new world order" to refer to a new period of history characterised by a dramatic change in world political thought and in the balance of power after World War I and World War II. They all saw the period as an opportunity to implement idealistic proposals for global governance in the sense of new collective efforts to address worldwide problems that go beyond the capacity of individual nation-states to solve, while always respecting the right of nations to self-determination. These proposals led to the formation of international organizations, and international regimes and the General Agreement on Tariffs and Trade), which were calculated both to maintain a balance of power in favor of the United States and to regularize cooperation between nations, in order to achieve a peaceful phase of capitalism. These creations in particular and liberal internationalism in general, however, were regularly criticized and opposed by American paleoconservative business nationalists from the 1930s on.

Progressives welcomed these new international organizations and regimes in the aftermath of the two World Wars, but argued that they suffered from a democratic deficit and were therefore inadequate not only to prevent another global war but to foster global justice. The United Nations was designed in 1945 by US bankers and State Department planners, and was always intended to remain a free association of sovereign nation-states, not a transition to democratic world government. Thus, activists around the globe formed a world federalist movement, hoping in vain to create a "real" new world order.

British writer and futurist H. G. Wells went further than progressives in the 1940s, by appropriating and redefining the term "new world order" as a synonym for the establishment of a technocratic world state and of a planned economy. Despite the popularity of his ideas in some state-socialist circles, Wells failed to exert a deeper and more lasting influence because he was unable to concentrate his energies on a direct appeal to the intelligentsias who would ultimately have to coordinate a Wellsian new world order.

During the Red Scare of 1947–1957, agitators of the American secular and Christian right, influenced by the work of Canadian conspiracy theorist William Guy Carr, increasingly embraced and spread unfounded fears of Freemasons, Illuminati and Jews as the alleged driving forces behind an "international communist conspiracy". The threat of "Godless communism", in the form of a state atheistic and bureaucratic collectivist world government, demonized as the "Red Menace", therefore became the focus of apocalyptic millenarian conspiracism. The Red Scare came to shape one of the core ideas of the political right in the United States, which is that liberals and progressives, with their welfare-state policies and international cooperation programs such as foreign aid, supposedly contribute to a gradual process of collectivism that will inevitably lead to nations being replaced with a communist one-world government.

Right-wing populist advocacy groups with a paleoconservative world-view, such as the John Birch Society, disseminated a multitude of conspiracy theories in the 1960s claiming that the governments of both the United States and the Soviet Union were controlled by a cabal of corporate internationalists, greedy bankers and corrupt politicians who were intent on using the U.N. as the vehicle to create a "One World Government". This right-wing anti-globalist conspiracism fuelled the Bircher campaign for US withdrawal from the UN. American writer Mary M. Davison, in her 1966 booklet The Profound Revolution, traced the alleged New World Order conspiracy to the establishment of the US Federal Reserve in 1913 by international bankers, whom she claimed later formed the Council on Foreign Relations in 1921 as a shadow government. At the time the booklet was published, many readers would have interpreted "international bankers" as a reference to a postulated "international Jewish banking conspiracy" masterminded by the Rothschilds.

Claiming that the term "New World Order" is used by a secretive elite dedicated to the destruction of all national sovereignties, American writer Gary Allen—in his books None Dare Call It Conspiracy, Rockefeller: Campaigning for the New World Order, and Say "No!" to the New World Order —articulated the anti-globalist theme of much current right-wing populist conspiracism in the US. Thus, after the fall of communism in the early 1990s, the main demonized scapegoat of the American far right shifted seamlessly from crypto-communists, who plotted on behalf of the Red Menace, to globalists, plotting on behalf of the New World Order. The relatively painless nature of the shift was due to growing right-wing populist opposition to corporate internationalism, but also in part to the basic underlying apocalyptic millenarian paradigm, which fed the Cold War and the witch-hunts of the McCarthy period.

In his speech, Toward a New World Order, delivered on 11 September 1990 during a joint session of the US Congress, President George H. W. Bush described his objectives for post-Cold War global governance in cooperation with post-Soviet states. He stated:

The New York Times observed that progressives were denouncing this new world order as a rationalization of American imperial ambitions in the Middle East, while conservatives rejected any new security arrangements altogether and fulminated about any possibility of a UN revival. Chip Berlet, an American investigative reporter specializing in the study of right-wing movements in the US, wrote that the Christian and secular hard right were especially terrified by the speech. Fundamentalist Christian groups interpreted Bush's words as signaling the End Times, while secular theorists approached it from an anti-communist and anti-collectivist standpoint and feared for a hegemony over all countries by the United Nations.}}

American televangelist Pat Robertson, with his 1991 best-selling book The New World Order, became the most prominent Christian popularizer of conspiracy theories about recent American history. He describes a scenario where Wall Street, the Federal Reserve System, the Council on Foreign Relations, the Bilderberg Group and the Trilateral Commission control the flow of events from behind the scenes, nudging people constantly and covertly in the direction of world government for the Antichrist.

Observers note that the galvanizing of right-wing populist conspiracy theorists such as Linda Thompson, Mark Koernke and Robert K. Spear into militancy led to the rise of the militia movement, which spread its anti-government ideology through speeches at rallies and meetings, books and videotapes sold at gun shows, shortwave and satellite radio, fax networks and computer bulletin boards. However, it is overnight AM radio shows and viral propaganda on the Internet that have most effectively contributed to their extremist political ideas about the New World Order finding their way into the previously apolitical literature of numerous Kennedy assassinologists, ufologists, lost land theorists and, most recently, occultists. From the mid–1990s on, the worldwide appeal of those subcultures transmitted New World Order conspiracism like a "mind virus" to a large new audience of seekers of stigmatized knowledge.

Hollywood conspiracy-thriller television shows and films also played a role in introducing a vast popular audience to various fringe theories related to New World Order conspiracism—black helicopters, FEMA "concentration camps", etc.— theories which for decades previously were confined to radical right-wing subcultures. The 1993–2002 television series The X-Files, the 1997 film Conspiracy Theory and the 1998 film The X-Files: Fight the Future are often cited as notable examples.

Following the start of the 21st century, and specifically during the late-2000s financial crisis, many politicians and pundits, such as Gordon Brown and Henry Kissinger, used the term "new world order" in their advocacy for a comprehensive reform of the global financial system and their calls for a "New Bretton Woods" taking into account emerging markets such as China and India. These declarations had the unintended consequence of providing fresh fodder for New World Order conspiracism, which culminated in talk-show host Sean Hannity stating on his Fox News Channel program Hannity that the "conspiracy theorists were right". Progressive media-watchdog groups have repeatedly criticized Fox News in general and its opinion show Glenn Beck in particular for not only mainstreaming the New World Order conspiracy theories of the radical right, but possibly agitating its lone wolves into action.

In 2009 American film directors Luke Meyer and Andrew Neel released New World Order, a critically acclaimed documentary film which explores the world of conspiracy theorists - such as American radio host Alex Jones - who consistently expose and vigorously oppose what they perceive as an emerging New World Order. The growing dissemination and popularity of conspiracy theories has also created an alliance between right-wing populist agitators and hip hop music's left-wing populist rappers , thus illustrating how anti-elitist conspiracism can create unlikely political allies in efforts to oppose a political system.

Conspiracy theories

There are numerous systemic conspiracy theories through which the concept of a New World Order is viewed. The following is a list of the major ones in roughly chronological order:

Since the 19th century, many apocalyptic millennial Christian eschatologists, starting with John Nelson Darby, have predicted a globalist conspiracy to impose a tyrannical New World Order governing structure as the fulfillment of prophecies about the "end time" in the Bible, specifically in the Book of Ezekiel, the Book of

Daniel, the Olivet discourse found in the Synoptic Gospels and the Book of Revelation. They claim that people who have made a deal with the Devil to gain wealth and power have become pawns in a supernatural chess game to move humanity into accepting a utopian world government that rests on the spiritual foundations of a syncretic-messianic world religion, which will later reveal itself to be a dystopian world empire that imposes the imperial cult of an "Unholy Trinity" of Satan, the Antichrist and the False Prophet. In many contemporary Christian conspiracy theories, the False Prophet will be either the last pope of the Catholic Church , a guru from the New Age movement, or even the leader of an elite fundamentalist Christian organization like the Fellowship, while the Antichrist will be either the President of the European Union, the Secretary-General of the United Nations, or even the Caliph of a pan-Islamic state.

Some of the most vocal critics of end-time conspiracy theories come from within Christianity. In 1993, historian Bruce Barron wrote a stern rebuke of apocalyptic Christian conspiracism in the Christian Research Journal, when reviewing Robertson's 1991 book The New World Order. Another critique can be found in historian Gregory S. Camp's 1997 book Selling Fear: Conspiracy Theories and End-Times Paranoia. Religious studies scholar Richard T. Hughes argues that "New World Order" rhetoric libels the Christian faith, since the "New World Order" as defined by Christian conspiracy theorists has no basis in the Bible whatsoever. Furthermore, he argues that not only is this idea unbiblical, it is positively anti-biblical and fundamentally anti-Christian, because by misinterpreting key passages in the Book of Revelation, it turns a comforting message about the coming kingdom of God into one of fear, panic and despair in the face of an allegedly approaching one-world government. Progressive Christians, such as preacher-theologian Peter J. Gomes, caution Christian fundamentalists that a "spirit of fear" can distort scripture and history through dangerously combining biblical literalism, apocalyptic timetables, demonization and oppressive prejudices, while Camp warns of the "very real danger that Christians could pick up some extra spiritual baggage" by credulously embracing conspiracy theories. They therefore call on Christians who indulge in conspiracism to repent.

Freemasonry is one of the world's oldest secular fraternal organizations and arose during late 16th–early 17th century Britain. Over the years a number of allegations and conspiracy theories have been directed towards Freemasonry, including the allegation that Freemasons have a hidden political agenda and are conspiring to bring about a New World Order, a world government organized according to Masonic principles and/or governed only by Freemasons.

The esoteric nature of Masonic symbolism and rites led to Freemasons first being accused of secretly practising Satanism in the late 18th century. The original allegation of a conspiracy within Freemasonry to subvert religions and governments in order to take over the world traces back to Scottish author John Robison, whose reactionary conspiracy theories crossed the Atlantic and influenced outbreaks of Protestant anti-Masonry in the United States during the 19th century. In the 1890s, French writer Léo Taxil wrote a series of pamphlets and books denouncing Freemasonry and charging their lodges with worshiping Lucifer as the Supreme Being and Great Architect of the Universe. Despite the fact that Taxil admitted that his claims were all a hoax, they were and still are believed and repeated by numerous conspiracy theorists and had a huge influence on subsequent anti-Masonic claims about Freemasonry.

Some conspiracy theorists eventually speculated that some Founding Fathers of the United States, such as George Washington and Benjamin Franklin, were having Masonic sacred geometric designs interwoven into American society, particularly in the Great Seal of the United States, the United States one-dollar bill, the architecture of National Mall landmarks and the streets and highways of Washington, D.C., as part of a master plan to create the first "Masonic government" as a model for the coming New World Order.

Freemasons rebut these claims of a Masonic conspiracy. Freemasonry, which promotes rationalism, places no power in occult symbols themselves, and it is not a part of its principles to view the drawing of symbols, no matter how large, as an act of consolidating or controlling power. Furthermore, there is no published information establishing the Masonic membership of the men responsible for the design of the Great Seal. While conspiracy theorists assert that there are elements of Masonic influence on the Great Seal of the United States, and that these elements were intentionally or unintentionally used because the creators were familiar with the symbols, in fact, the all-seeing Eye of Providence and the unfinished pyramid were symbols used as much outside Masonic lodges as within them in the late 18th century, therefore the designers were drawing from common esoteric symbols. The Latin phrase "novus ordo seclorum", appearing on the reverse side of the Great Seal since 1782 and on the back of the one-dollar bill since 1935, translates to "New Order of the Ages", and alludes to the beginning of an era where the United States of America is an independent nation-state; it is often mistranslated by conspiracy theorists as "New World Order".

Although the European continental branch of Freemasonry has organizations that allow political discussion within their Masonic Lodges, Masonic researcher Trevor W. McKeown argues that the accusations ignore several facts. Firstly, the many Grand Lodges are independent and sovereign, meaning they act on their own and do not have a common agenda. The points of belief of the various lodges often differ. Secondly, famous individual Freemasons have always held views that span the political spectrum and show no particular pattern or preference. As such, the term "Masonic government" is erroneous; there is no consensus among Freemasons about what an ideal government would look like.

The Order of the Illuminati was an Enlightenment-age secret society founded by university professor Adam Weishaupt on 1 May 1776, in Upper Bavaria, Germany. The movement consisted of advocates of freethought, secularism, liberalism, republicanism, and gender equality, recruited from the German Masonic Lodges, who sought to teach rationalism through mystery schools. In 1785, the order was infiltrated, broken up and suppressed by the government agents of Charles Theodore, Elector of Bavaria, in his preemptive campaign to neutralize the threat of secret societies ever becoming hotbeds of conspiracies to overthrow the Bavarian monarchy and its state religion, Roman Catholicism. There is no evidence that the Bavarian Illuminati survived its suppression in 1785.

In the late 18th century, reactionary conspiracy theorists, such as Scottish physicist John Robison and French Jesuit priest Augustin Barruel, began speculating that the Illuminati had survived their suppression and become the masterminds behind the French Revolution and the Reign of Terror. The Illuminati were accused of being subversives who were attempting to secretly orchestrate a revolutionary wave in Europe and the rest of the world in order to spread the most radical ideas and movements of the Enlightenment—anti-clericalism, anti-monarchism, and anti-patriarchalism—and to create a world noocracy and cult of reason. During the 19th century, fear of an Illuminati conspiracy was a real concern of the European ruling classes, and their oppressive reactions to this unfounded fear provoked in 1848 the very revolutions they sought to prevent.

During the interwar period of the 20th century, fascist propagandists, such as British revisionist historian Nesta Helen Webster and American socialite Edith Starr Miller, not only popularized the myth of an Illuminati conspiracy but claimed that it was a subversive secret society which served the Jewish elites that supposedly propped up both finance capitalism and Soviet communism in order to divide and rule the world. American evangelist Gerald Burton Winrod and other conspiracy theorists within the fundamentalist Christian movement in the United States—which emerged in the 1910s as a backlash against the principles of Enlightenment secular humanism, modernism, and liberalism—became the main channel of dissemination of Illuminati conspiracy theories in the U.S.. Right-wing populists, such as members of the John Birch Society, subsequently began speculating that some collegiate fraternities , gentlemen's clubs , and think tanks of the American upper class are front organizations of the Illuminati, which they accuse of plotting to create a New World Order through a one-world government.

The Protocols of the Elders of Zion is an antisemitic canard, originally published in Russian in 1903, alleging a Judeo-Masonic conspiracy to achieve world domination. The text purports to be the minutes of the secret meetings of a cabal of Jewish masterminds, which has co-opted Freemasonry and is plotting to rule the world on behalf of all Jews because they believe themselves to be the chosen people of God. The Protocols incorporate many of the core conspiracist themes outlined in the Robison and Barruel attacks on the Freemasons, and overlay them with antisemitic allegations about anti-Tsarist movements in Russia. The Protocols reflect themes similar to more general critiques of Enlightenment liberalism by conservative aristocrats who support monarchies and state religions. The interpretation intended by the publication of The Protocols is that if one peels away the layers of the Masonic conspiracy, past the Illuminati, one finds the rotten Jewish core.

Numerous polemicists, such as Irish journalist Philip Graves in a 1921 article in The Times, and British academic Norman Cohn in his 1967 book Warrant for Genocide, have proven The Protocols to be both a hoax and a clear case of plagiarism. There is general agreement that Russian-French writer and political activist Matvei Golovinski fabricated the text for Okhrana, the secret police of the Russian Empire, as a work of counter-revolutionary propaganda prior to the 1905 Russian Revolution, by plagiarizing, almost word for word in some passages, from The Dialogue in Hell Between Machiavelli and Montesquieu, a 19th-century satire against Napoleon III of France written by French political satirist and Legitimist militant Maurice Joly.

Responsible for feeding many antisemitic and anti-Masonic mass hysterias of the 20th century, The Protocols has been influential in the development of some conspiracy theories, including some New World Order theories, and appears repeatedly in certain contemporary conspiracy literature. For example, the authors of the 1982 controversial book The Holy Blood and the Holy Grail concluded that The Protocols was the most persuasive piece of evidence for the existence and activities of the Priory of Sion. They speculated that this secret society was working behind the scenes to establish a theocratic "United States of Europe". Politically and religiously unified through the imperial cult of a Merovingian Great Monarch—supposedly descended from a Jesus bloodline—who occupies both the throne of Europe and the Holy See, this "Holy European Empire" would become the hyperpower of the 21st century. Although the Priory of Sion itself has been exhaustively debunked by journalists and scholars as a hoax, some apocalyptic millenarian Christian eschatologists who believe The Protocols is authentic became convinced that the Priory of Sion was a fulfillment of prophecies found in the Book of Revelation and further proof of an anti-Christian conspiracy of epic proportions signaling the imminence of a New World Order.

Skeptics argue that the current gambit of contemporary conspiracy theorists who use The Protocols is to claim that they "really" come from some group other than the Jews, such as fallen angels or alien invaders. Although it is hard to determine whether the conspiracy-minded actually believe this or are simply trying to sanitize a discredited text, skeptics argue that it does not make much difference, since they leave the actual, antisemitic text unchanged. The result is to give The Protocols credibility and circulation.

During the second half of Britain's "imperial century" between 1815 and 1914, English-born South African businessman, mining magnate and politician Cecil Rhodes advocated the British Empire reannexing the United States of America and reforming itself into an "Imperial Federation" to bring about a hyperpower and lasting world peace. In his first will, written in 1877 at the age of 23, he expressed his wish to fund a secret society that would advance this goal:

In 1890, thirteen years after "his now famous will," Rhodes elaborated on the same idea: establishment of "England everywhere," which would "ultimately lead to the cessation of all wars, and one language throughout the world." "The only thing feasible to carry out this idea is a secret society gradually absorbing the wealth of the world to be devoted to such an object."

Rhodes also concentrated on the Rhodes Scholarship, which had British statesman Alfred Milner as one of its trustees. Established in 1902, the original goal of the trust fund was to foster peace among the great powers by creating a sense of fraternity and a shared world view among future British, American, and German leaders by having enabled them to study for free at the University of Oxford.

Milner and British official Lionel George Curtis were the architects of the Round Table movement, a network of organizations promoting closer union between Britain and its self-governing colonies. To this end, Curtis founded the Royal Institute of International Affairs in June 1919 and, with his 1938 book The Commonwealth of God, began advocating for the creation of an imperial federation that eventually reannexes the U.S., which would be presented to Protestant churches as being the work of the Christian God to elicit their support. The Commonwealth of Nations was created in 1949 but it would only be a free association of independent states rather than the powerful imperial federation imagined by Rhodes, Milner and Curtis.

The Council on Foreign Relations began in 1917 with a group of New York academics who were asked by President Woodrow Wilson to offer options for the foreign policy of the United States in the interwar period. Originally envisioned as a group of American and British scholars and diplomats, some of whom belonging to the Round Table movement, it was a subsequent group of 108 New York financiers, manufacturers and international lawyers organized in June 1918 by Nobel Peace Prize recipient and U.S. secretary of state Elihu Root, that became the Council on Foreign Relations on 29 July 1921. The first of the council's projects was a quarterly journal launched in September 1922, called Foreign Affairs. The Trilateral Commission was founded in July 1973, at the initiative of American banker David Rockefeller, who was chairman of the Council on Foreign Relations at that time. It is a private organization established to foster closer cooperation among the United States, Europe and Japan. The Trilateral Commission is widely seen as a counterpart to the Council on Foreign Relations.

In the 1960s, right-wing populist individuals and groups with a paleoconservative worldview, such as members of the John Birch Society, were the first to combine and spread a business nationalist critique of corporate internationalists networked through think tanks such as the Council on Foreign Relations with a grand conspiracy theory casting them as front organizations for the Round Table of the "Anglo-American Establishment", which are financed by an "international banking cabal" that has supposedly been plotting from the late 19th century on to impose an oligarchic new world order through a global financial system. Anti-globalist conspiracy theorists therefore fear that international bankers are planning to eventually subvert the independence of the U.S. by subordinating national sovereignty to a strengthened Bank for International Settlements.

The research findings of historian Carroll Quigley, author of the 1966 book Tragedy and Hope, are taken by both conspiracy theorists of the American Old Right and New Left to substantiate this view, even though Quigley argued that the Establishment is not involved in a plot to implement a one-world government but rather British and American benevolent imperialism driven by the mutual interests of economic elites in the United Kingdom and the United States. Quigley also argued that, although the Round Table still exists today, its position in influencing the policies of world leaders has been much reduced from its heyday during World War I and slowly waned after the end of World War II and the Suez Crisis. Today the Round Table is largely a ginger group, designed to consider and gradually influence the policies of the Commonwealth of Nations, but faces strong opposition. Furthermore, in American society after 1965, the problem, according to Quigley, was that no elite was in charge and acting responsibly.

Larry McDonald, the second president of the John Birch Society and a conservative Democratic member of the United States House of Representatives who represented the 7th congressional district of Georgia, wrote a foreword for

Allen's 1976 book The Rockefeller File, wherein he claimed that the Rockefellers and their allies were driven by a desire to create a one-world government that combined "super-capitalism" with communism and would be fully under their control. He saw a conspiracy plot that was "international in scope, generations old in planning, and incredibly evil in intent."

In his 2002 autobiography Memoirs, David Rockefeller wrote:

Barkun argues that this statement is partly facetious and partly serious—the desire to encourage trilateral cooperation among the U.S., Europe, and Japan, for example—an ideal that used to be a hallmark of the internationalist wing of the Republican Party when there was an internationalist wing. The statement, however, is taken at face value and widely cited by conspiracy theorists as proof that the Council on Foreign Relations uses its role as the brain trust of American presidents, senators and representatives to manipulate them into supporting a New World Order in the form of a one-world government.

In a 13 November 2007 interview with Canadian journalist Benjamin Fulford, Rockefeller countered that he felt no need for a world government and wished for the governments of the world to work together and collaborate. He also stated that it seemed neither likely nor desirable to have only one elected government rule the whole world. He criticized accusations of him being "ruler of the world" as nonsensical.

Some American social critics, such as Laurence H. Shoup, argue that the Council on Foreign Relations is an "imperial brain trust" which has, for decades, played a central behind-the-scenes role in shaping U.S. foreign policy choices for the post-World War II international order and the Cold War by determining what options show up on the agenda and what options do not even make it to the table; others, such as G. William Domhoff, argue that it is in fact a mere policy discussion forum which provides the business input to U.S. foreign policy planning. Domhoff argues that "t has nearly 3,000 members, far too many for secret plans to be kept within the group. All the council does is sponsor discussion groups, debates and speakers. As far as being secretive, it issues annual reports and allows access to its historical archives." However, all these critics agree that "istorical studies of the CFR show that it has a very different role in the overall power structure than what is claimed by conspiracy theorists."

In his 1928 book The Open Conspiracy British writer and futurist H. G. Wells promoted cosmopolitanism and offered blueprints for a world revolution and world brain to establish a technocratic world state and planned economy. Wells warned, however, in his 1940 book The New World Order that:

Wells's books were influential in giving a second meaning to the term "new world order", which would only be used by state socialist supporters and anti-communist opponents for generations to come. However, despite the popularity and notoriety of his ideas, Wells failed to exert a deeper and more lasting influence because he was unable to concentrate his energies on a direct appeal to intelligentsias who would, ultimately, have to coordinate the Wellsian new world order.

British neo-Theosophical occultist Alice Bailey, one of the founders of the so-called New Age movement, prophesied in 1940 the eventual victory of the Allies of World War II over the Axis powers and the establishment by the Allies of a political and religious New World Order. She saw a federal world government as the culmination of Wells' Open Conspiracy but favorably argued that it would be synarchist because it was guided by the Masters of the Ancient Wisdom, intent on preparing humanity for the mystical second coming of Christ, and the dawning of the Age of Aquarius. According to Bailey, a group of ascended masters called the Great White Brotherhood works on the "inner planes" to oversee the transition to the New World Order but, for now, the members of this Spiritual Hierarchy are only known to a few occult scientists, with whom they communicate telepathically, but as the need for their personal involvement in the plan increases, there will be an "Externalization of the Hierarchy" and everyone will know of their presence on Earth.

Bailey's writings, along with American writer Marilyn Ferguson's 1980 book The Aquarian Conspiracy, contributed to conspiracy theorists of the Christian right viewing the New Age movement as the "false religion" that would supersede Christianity in a New World Order. Skeptics argue that the term "New Age movement" is a misnomer, generally used by conspiracy theorists as a catch-all rubric for any new religious movement that is not fundamentalist Christian. By this logic, anything that is not Christian is by definition actively and willfully anti-Christian.

Paradoxically, since the first decade of the 21st century, New World Order conspiracism is increasingly being embraced and propagandized by New Age occultists, who are people bored by rationalism and drawn to stigmatized knowledge—such as alternative medicine, astrology, quantum mysticism, spiritualism, and theosophy. Thus, New Age conspiracy theorists, such as the makers of documentary films like Esoteric Agenda, claim that globalists who plot on behalf of the New World Order are simply misusing occultism for Machiavellian ends, such as adopting 21 December 2012 as the exact date for the establishment of the New World Order for the purpose of taking advantage of the growing 2012 phenomenon, which has its origins in the fringe Mayanist theories of New Age writers José Argüelles, Terence McKenna, and Daniel Pinchbeck.

Skeptics argue that the connection of conspiracy theorists and occultists follows from their common fallacious premises. First, any widely accepted belief must necessarily be false. Second, stigmatized knowledge—what the Establishment spurns—must be true. The result is a large, self-referential network in which, for example, some UFO religionists promote anti-Jewish phobias while some antisemites practice Peruvian shamanism.

Conspiracy theorists often use the term "Fourth Reich" simply as a pejorative synonym for the "New World Order" to imply that its state ideology and government will be similar to Germany's Third Reich. However, some conspiracy theorists use the research findings of American journalist Edwin Black, author of the 2009 book Nazi Nexus, to claim that some American corporations and philanthropic foundations—whose complicity was pivotal to the Third Reich's war effort, Nazi eugenics and the Holocaust—are now conspiring to build a Fourth Reich.

Conspiracy theorists, such as American writer Jim Marrs, claim that some ex-Nazis, who survived the fall of the Greater German Reich, along with sympathizers in the United States and elsewhere, given haven by organizations like ODESSA and Die Spinne, have been working behind the scenes since the end of World War II to enact at least some principles of Nazism into culture, government, and business worldwide, but primarily in the U.S. They cite the influence of ex-Nazi scientists brought in under Operation Paperclip to help advance aerospace manufacturing in the U.S. with technological principles from Nazi UFOs, and the acquisition and creation of conglomerates by ex-Nazis and their sympathizers after the war, in both Europe and the U.S.

This neo-Nazi conspiracy is said to be animated by an "Iron Dream" in which the American Empire, having thwarted the Judeo-Masonic conspiracy and overthrown its Zionist Occupation Government, gradually establishes a Fourth Reich formerly known as the "Western Imperium"—a pan-Aryan world empire modeled after Adolf Hitler's New Order—which reverses the "decline of the West" and ushers a golden age of white supremacy.

Skeptics argue that conspiracy theorists grossly overestimate the influence of ex-Nazis and neo-Nazis on American society, and point out that political repression at home and imperialism abroad have a long history in the United States that predates the 20th century. Some political scientists, such as Sheldon Wolin, have expressed concern that the twin forces of democratic deficit and superpower status have paved the way in the U.S. for the emergence of an inverted totalitarianism which contradicts many principles of Nazism.

Since the late 1970s, extraterrestrials from other habitable planets or parallel dimensions and intraterrestrials from Hollow Earth have been included in the New World Order conspiracy, in more or less dominant roles, as in the theories put forward by American writers Stan Deyo and Milton William Cooper, and British writer David Icke.

The common theme in these conspiracy theories is that aliens have been among us for decades, centuries or millennia, but a government cover-up enforced by "Men in Black" has shielded the public from knowledge of a secret alien invasion. Motivated by speciesism and imperialism, these aliens have been and are secretly manipulating developments and changes in human society in order to more efficiently control and exploit human beings. In some theories, alien infiltrators have shapeshifted into human form and move freely throughout human society, even to the point of taking control of command positions in governmental, corporate, and religious institutions, and are now in the final stages of their plan to take over the world. A mythical covert government agency of the United States code-named Majestic 12 is often imagined being the shadow government which collaborates with the alien occupation and permits alien abductions, in exchange for assistance in the development and testing of military "flying saucers" at Area 51, in order for United States armed forces to achieve full-spectrum dominance.

Skeptics, who adhere to the psychosocial hypothesis for unidentified flying objects, argue that the convergence of New World Order conspiracy theory and UFO conspiracy theory is a product of not only the era's widespread mistrust of governments and the popularity of the extraterrestrial hypothesis for UFOs but of the far right and ufologists actually joining forces. Barkun notes that the only positive side to this development is that, if conspirators plotting to rule the world are believed to be aliens, traditional human scapegoats are downgraded or exonerated.

Antiscience and neo-Luddite conspiracy theorists emphasize technology forecasting in their New World Order conspiracy theories. They speculate that the global power elite are reactionary modernists pursuing a transhumanist agenda to develop and use human enhancement technologies in order to become a "posthuman ruling caste", while change accelerates toward a technological singularity—a theorized future point of discontinuity when events will accelerate at such a pace that normal unenhanced humans will be unable to predict or even understand the rapid changes occurring in the world around them. Conspiracy theorists fear the outcome will either be the emergence of a Brave New World-like dystopia—a "Brave New World Order"—or the extinction of the human species.

Democratic transhumanists, such as American sociologist James Hughes, counter that many influential members of the United States Establishment are bioconservatives strongly opposed to human enhancement, as demonstrated by President Bush's Council on Bioethics's proposed international treaty prohibiting human cloning and germline engineering. Furthermore, he argues that conspiracy theorists underestimate how fringe the transhumanist movement really is.

Postulated implementations

Just as there are several overlapping or conflicting theories among conspiracists about the nature of the New World Order, so are there several beliefs about how its architects and planners will implement it:

Conspiracy theorists generally speculate that the New World Order is being implemented gradually, citing the formation of the U.S. Federal Reserve System in 1913; the League of Nations in 1919; the International Monetary Fund in 1944; the United Nations in 1945; the World Bank in 1945; the World Health Organization in 1948; the European Union and the euro currency in 1993; the World Trade Organization in 1998; the African Union in 2002; and the Union of South American Nations in 2008 as major milestones.

An increasingly popular conspiracy theory among American right-wing populists is that the hypothetical North American Union and the amero currency, proposed by the Council on Foreign Relations and its counterparts in Mexico and Canada, will be the next milestone in the implementation of the New World Order. The theory holds that a group of shadowy and mostly nameless international elites are planning to replace the federal government of the United States with a transnational government. Therefore, conspiracy theorists believe the borders between Mexico, Canada and the United States are in the process of being erased, covertly, by a group of globalists whose ultimate goal is to replace national governments in Washington, D.C., Ottawa and Mexico City with a European-style political union and a bloated E.U.-style bureaucracy.

Skeptics argue that the North American Union exists only as a proposal contained in one of a thousand academic and/or policy papers published each year that advocate all manner of idealistic but ultimately unrealistic approaches to social, economic and political problems. Most of these are passed around in their own circles and eventually filed away and forgotten by junior staffers in congressional offices. Some of these papers, however, become touchstones for the conspiracy-minded and form the basis of all kinds of unfounded xenophobic fears especially during times of economic anxiety.

For example, in March 2009, as a result of the late-2000s financial crisis, the People's Republic of China and the Russian Federation pressed for urgent consideration of a new international reserve currency and the United Nations Conference on Trade and Development proposed greatly expanding the I.M.F.'s special drawing rights. Conspiracy theorists fear these proposals are a call for the U.S. to adopt a single global currency for a New World Order.

Judging that both national governments and global institutions have proven ineffective in addressing worldwide problems that go beyond the capacity of individual nation-states to solve, some political scientists critical of New World Order conspiracism, such as Mark C. Partridge, argue that regionalism will be the major force in the coming decades, pockets of power around regional centers: Western Europe around Brussels, the Western Hemisphere around Washington, D.C., East Asia around Beijing, and Eastern Europe around Moscow. As such, the E.U., the Shanghai Cooperation Organisation, and the G-20 will likely become more influential as time progresses. The question then is not whether global governance is gradually emerging, but rather how will these regional powers interact with one another.

American right-wing populist conspiracy theorists, especially those who joined the militia movement in the United States, speculate that the New World Order will be implemented through a dramatic coup d'état by a "secret team", using black helicopters, in the U.S. and other nation-states to bring about a totalitarian world government controlled by the United Nations and enforced by troops of foreign U.N. peacekeepers. Following the Rex 84 and Operation Garden Plot plans, this military coup would involve the suspension of the Constitution, the imposition of martial law, and the appointment of military commanders to head state and local governments and to detain dissidents.

These conspiracy theorists, who are all strong believers in a right to keep and bear arms, are extremely fearful that the passing of any gun control legislation will be later followed by the abolishment of personal gun ownership and a campaign of gun confiscation, and that the refugee camps of emergency management agencies such as FEMA will be used for the internment of suspected subversives, making little effort to distinguish true threats to the New World Order from pacifist dissidents.

Before year 2000 some survivalists wrongly believed this process would be set in motion by the predicted Y2K problem causing societal collapse. Since many left-wing and right-wing conspiracy theorists believe that the 11 September attacks were a false flag operation carried out by the United States intelligence community, as part of a strategy of tension to justify political repression at home and preemptive war abroad, they have become convinced that a more catastrophic terrorist incident will be responsible for triggering Executive Directive 51 in order to complete the transition to a police state.

Skeptics argue that unfounded fears about an imminent or eventual gun ban, military coup, internment, or U.N. invasion and occupation are rooted in the siege mentality of the American militia movement but also an apocalyptic millenarianism which provides a basic narrative within the political right in the U.S., claiming that the idealized society is thwarted by subversive conspiracies of liberal secular humanists who want "Big Government" and globalists who plot on behalf of the New World Order.

Conspiracy theorists concerned with surveillance abuse believe that the New World Order is being implemented by the cult of intelligence at the core of the surveillance-industrial complex through mass surveillance and the use of Social Security numbers, the bar-coding of retail goods with Universal Product Code markings, and, most recently, RFID tagging by microchip implants.

Claiming that corporations and government are planning to track every move of consumers and citizens with RFID as the latest step toward a 1984-like surveillance state, consumer privacy advocates, such as Katherine Albrecht and Liz McIntyre, have become Christian conspiracy theorists who believe spychips must be resisted because they argue that modern database and communications technologies, coupled with point of sale data-capture equipment and sophisticated ID and authentication systems, now make it possible to require a biometrically associated number or mark to make purchases. They fear that the ability to implement such a system closely resembles the Number of the Beast prophesied in the Book of Revelation.

In January 2002, the Information Awareness Office was established by the Defense Advanced Research Projects Agency to bring together several DARPA projects focused on applying information technology to counter asymmetric threats to national security. Following public criticism that the development and deployment of these technologies could potentially lead to a mass surveillance system, the IAO was defunded by the United States Congress in 2003. The second source of controversy involved IAO's original logo, which depicted the "all-seeing" Eye of Providence atop of a pyramid looking down over the globe, accompanied by the Latin phrase scientia est potentia . Although DARPA eventually removed the logo from its website, it left a lasting impression on privacy advocates. It also inflamed conspiracy theorists, who misinterpret the "eye and pyramid" as the Masonic symbol of the Illuminati, an 18th-century secret society they speculate continues to exist and is plotting on behalf of a New World Order.

American historian Richard Landes, who specializes in the history of apocalypticism and was co-founder and director of the Center for Millennial Studies at Boston University, argues that new and emerging technologies often trigger alarmism among millenarians and even the introduction of Gutenberg's printing press in 1436 caused waves of apocalyptic thinking. The Year 2000 problem, bar codes and Social Security numbers all triggered end-time warnings which either proved to be false or simply were no longer taken seriously once the public became accustomed to these technological changes. Civil libertarians argue that the privatization of surveillance and the rise of the surveillance-industrial complex in the United States does raise legitimate concerns about the erosion of privacy. However, skeptics of mass surveillance conspiracism caution that such concerns should be disentangled from secular paranoia about Big Brother or religious hysteria about the Antichrist.

Conspiracy theorists of the Christian right, starting with British revisionist historian Nesta Helen Webster, believe there is an ancient occult conspiracy—started by the first mystagogues of Gnosticism and perpetuated by their alleged esoteric successors, such as the Kabbalists, Cathars, Knights Templar, Hermeticists, Rosicrucians, Freemasons, and, ultimately, the Illuminati—which seeks to subvert the Judeo-Christian foundations of the Western world and implement the New World Order through a one-world religion that prepares the masses to embrace the imperial cult of the Antichrist. More broadly, they speculate that globalists who plot on behalf of a New World Order are directed by occult agencies of some sort: unknown superiors, spiritual hierarchies, demons, fallen angels and/or Lucifer. They believe that these conspirators use the power of occult sciences, symbols, rituals, monuments, buildings and facilities to advance their plot to rule the world.

For example, in June 1979, an unknown benefactor under the pseudonym "R. C. Christian" had a huge granite megalith built in the U.S. state of Georgia, which acts like a compass, calendar, and clock. A message comprising ten guides is inscribed on the occult structure in many languages to serve as instructions for survivors of a doomsday event to establish a more enlightened and sustainable civilization than the one which was destroyed. The "Georgia Guidestones" have subsequently become a spiritual and political Rorschach test onto which any number of ideas can be imposed. Some New Agers and neo-pagans revere it as a ley-line power nexus while a few conspiracy theorists are convinced that they are engraved with the New World Order's anti-Christian "Ten Commandments." Should the Guidestones survive for centuries as their creators intended, many more meanings could arise, equally unrelated to the designer's original intention.

Skeptics argue that the demonization of Western esotericism by conspiracy theorists is rooted in religious intolerance but also in the same moral panics that have fueled witch trials in the Early Modern period, and satanic ritual abuse allegations in the United States.

Conspiracy theorists believe that the New World Order will also be implemented through the use of human population control in order to more easily monitor and control the movement of individuals. The means range from stopping the growth of human societies through reproductive health and family planning programs, which promote abstinence, contraception and abortion, or intentionally reducing the bulk of the world population through genocides by mongering unnecessary wars, through plagues by engineering emergent viruses and tainting vaccines, and through environmental disasters by controlling the weather , etc. Conspiracy theorists argue that globalists plotting on behalf of a New World Order are neo-Malthusians who engage in overpopulation and climate change alarmism in order to create public support for coercive population control and ultimately world government. Agenda 21 is condemned as "reconcentrating" people into urban areas and depopulating rural ones, even generating a dystopian novel by Glenn Beck where single-family homes are a distant memory.

Skeptics argue that fears of population control can be traced back to the traumatic legacy of the eugenics movement's "war against the weak" in the United States during the first decades of the 20th century but also the Second Red Scare in the U.S. during the late 1940s and 1950s, and to a lesser extent in the 1960s, when activists on the far right of American politics routinely opposed public health programs, notably water fluoridation, mass vaccination and mental health services, by asserting they were all part of a far-reaching plot to impose a socialist or communist regime. Their views were influenced by opposition to a number of major social and political changes that had happened in recent years: the growth of internationalism, particularly the United Nations and its programs; the introduction of social welfare provisions, particularly the various programs established by the New Deal; and government efforts to reduce inequalities in the social structure of the U.S..

Social critics accuse governments, corporations, and the mass media of being involved in the manufacturing of a national consensus and, paradoxically, a culture of fear due to the potential for increased social control that a mistrustful and mutually fearing population might offer to those in power. The worst fear of some conspiracy theorists, however, is that the New World Order will be implemented through the use of mind control—a broad range of tactics able to subvert an individual's control of his or her own thinking, behavior, emotions, or decisions.

These tactics are said to include everything from Manchurian candidate-style brainwashing of sleeper agents to engineering psychological operations and parapsychological operations to influence the masses. The concept of wearing a tin foil hat for protection from such threats has become a popular stereotype and term of derision; the phrase serves as a byword for paranoia and is associated with conspiracy theorists.

Skeptics argue that the paranoia behind a conspiracy theorist's obsession with mind control, population control, occultism, surveillance abuse, Big Business, Big Government, and globalization arises from a combination of two factors, when he or she: 1) holds strong individualist values and 2) lacks power. The first attribute refers to people who care deeply about an individual's right to make their own choices and direct their own lives without interference or obligations to a larger system , but combine this with a sense of powerlessness in one's own life, and one gets what some psychologists call "agency panic," intense anxiety about an apparent loss of autonomy to outside forces or regulators. When fervent individualists feel that they cannot exercise their independence, they experience a crisis and assume that larger forces are to blame for usurping this freedom.

Alleged conspirators

According to Domhoff, many people seem to believe that the United States is ruled from behind the scenes by a conspiratorial elite with secret desires, i.e., by a small secretive group that wants to change the government system or put the country under the control of a world government. In the past the conspirators were usually said to be crypto-communists who were intent upon bringing the United States under a common world government with the Soviet Union, but the dissolution of the USSR in 1991 undercut that theory. Domhoff notes that most conspiracy theorists changed their focus to the United Nations as the likely controlling force in a New World Order, an idea which is undermined by the powerlessness of the U.N. and the unwillingness of even moderates within the American Establishment to give it anything but a limited role.

Although skeptical of New World Order conspiracism, political scientist David Rothkopf argues, in the 2008 book Superclass: The Global Power Elite and the World They Are Making, that the world population of 6 billion people is governed by an elite of 6,000 individuals. Until the late 20th century, governments of the great powers provided most of the superclass, accompanied by a few heads of international movements and entrepreneurs . According to Rothkopf, in the early 21st century, economic clout—fueled by the explosive expansion of international trade, travel and communication—rules; the nation-state's power has diminished shrinking politicians to minority power broker status; leaders in international business, finance and the defense industry not only dominate the superclass, they move freely into high positions in their nations' governments and back to private life largely beyond the notice of elected legislatures, which remain abysmally ignorant of affairs beyond their borders. He asserts that the superclass' disproportionate influence over national policy is constructive but always self-interested, and that across the world, few object to corruption and oppressive governments provided they can do business in these countries.

Viewing the history of the world as the history of warfare between secret societies, conspiracy theorists go further than Rothkopf, and other scholars who have studied the global power elite, by claiming that established upper-class families with "old money" who founded and finance the Bilderberg Group, Bohemian Club, Club of Rome, Council on Foreign Relations, Rhodes Trust, Skull and Bones, Trilateral Commission, and similar think tanks and private clubs, are illuminated conspirators plotting to impose a totalitarian New World Order—the implementation of an authoritarian world government controlled by the United Nations and a global central bank, which maintains political power through the financialization of the economy, regulation and restriction of speech through the concentration of media ownership, mass surveillance, widespread use of state terrorism, and an all-encompassing propaganda that creates a cult of personality around a puppet world leader and ideologizes world government as the culmination of history's progress.

Marxists, who are skeptical of right-wing populist conspiracy theories, also accuse the global power elite of not having the best interests of all at heart, and many intergovernmental organizations of suffering from a democratic deficit, but they argue that the superclass are plutocrats only interested in brazenly imposing a neoliberal or neoconservative new world order—the implementation of global capitalism through economic and military coercion to protect the interests of transnational corporations—which systematically undermines the possibility of a socialist one-world government. Arguing that the world is in the middle of a transition from the American Empire to the rule of a global ruling class that has emerged from within the American Empire, they point out that right-wing populist conspiracy theorists, blinded by their anti-communism, fail to see is that what they demonize as the "New World Order" is, ironically, the highest stage of the very capitalist economic system they defend.

Criticism

Skeptics of New World Order conspiracy theories accuse its proponents of indulging in the furtive fallacy, a belief that significant facts of history are necessarily sinister; conspiracism, a world view that centrally places conspiracy theories in the unfolding of history, rather than social and economic forces; and fusion paranoia, a promiscuous absorption of fears from any source whatsoever.

Domhoff, a research professor in psychology and sociology who studies theories of power, writes in a March 2005 essay entitled There Are No Conspiracies:

Partridge, a contributing editor to the global affairs magazine Diplomatic Courier, writes in a December 2008 article entitled One World Government: Conspiracy Theory or Inevitable Future?:

Although some cultural critics see superconspiracy theories about a New World Order as "postmodern metanarratives" that may be politically empowering, a way of giving ordinary people a narrative structure with which to question what they see around them, skeptics argue that conspiracism leads people into cynicism, convoluted thinking, and a tendency to feel it is hopeless even as they denounce the alleged conspirators.

Alexander Zaitchik from the Southern Poverty Law Center wrote a report titled "'Patriot' Paranoia: A Look at the Top Ten Conspiracy Theories", in which he personally condemns such conspiracies as an effort of the radical right to undermine society.

Concerned that the improvisational millennialism of most conspiracy theories about a New World Order might motivate lone wolves to engage in leaderless resistance leading to domestic terrorist incidents like the Oklahoma City bombing, Barkun writes:

Warning of the threat to American democracy posed by right-wing populist movements led by demagogues who mobilize support for mob rule or even a fascist revolution by exploiting the fear of conspiracies, Berlet writes:

Hughes, a professor of religion, warns that no religious idea has greater potential for shaping global politics in profoundly negative ways than "the new world order". He writes in a February 2011 article entitled Revelation, Revolutions, and the Tyrannical New World Order:

Criticisms of New World Order conspiracy theorists also come from within their own community. Despite believing themselves to be "freedom fighters", many right-wing populist conspiracy theorists hold views that are incompatible with their professed libertarianism.

Printed in Great Britain
by Amazon